AMY'S ANSWERING MACHINE

Messages from Mom

AMY BORKOWSKY

Illustrated by Marty Bucella

POCKET BOOKS

New York London Toronto Sydney Singapore

POCKET BOOKS, a division of Simon & Schuster, Inc.
1230 Avenue of the Americas, New York, NY 10020

ISBN: 0-7434-2228-7

First Pocket Books hardcover printing April 2001

10   9   8   7   6   5   4

POCKET and colophon are registered trademarks of
Simon & Schuster, Inc.

Printed in the U.S.A.

To my sweet, loving mother
for making my life possible.

And at times, impossible.

Thanks for your care, your kindness,
and your inspiration.

THE MESSAGE
BEFORE
THE MESSAGES

· · · · · · · · · · · · · · · · · · ·

A lot of people who are driven to the point of insanity report hearing voices—voices commanding them to stalk, maim, or even kill.

Then there are people like you and me. We also hear voices that leave us at the brink of our sanity, only these voices are commanding us to zip up our jackets or eat enough roughage.

The voices *we* hear don't come from God but from someone much more powerful.

Our mothers.

The only difference between any other adult who's being driven nuts by her mother and me is that I just happened to have saved my mother's voice on the microcassettes from my answering machine.

In fact, I've been saving almost *all* my answering machine messages for well over a decade.

Recently, I released a CD of my mother's messages through my Website at sendamy.com. Judging by the flood of email I've been getting, I'm not alone in having a mother who uses the phone lines to stay way *too* connected—a mother who offers constant advice on what to eat, how to dress, and who to date.

It doesn't help that the phone companies have been fighting a rate war, resulting in long-distance charges as low as five cents a minute and local calling plans with unlimited usage. As in any war, who suffers the most? It's the children—people like you and me whose mothers now have *nothing* holding them back whenever The Urge to Call strikes.

With all the advances in telecommunications— from answering machines that our mothers "commandeer" to cell phones that let them track us wherever we go—it's not Big Brother watching over us.

It's Big Mother.

So allow me to take you on a journey to the land of Overprotection, as I share messages from a mother who seems to think the phone cord is an umbilical cord.

You'll notice that I make liberal use of phrases such as "I love my mother, but," "As much as we love our parents," and "I know my mother means well, but." Basically, these are road signs indicating Sharp Criticism Ahead, and I use them because I don't want to feel guilty.

And even though it's hard to remember sometimes, I use these phrases because they're true. I do know how lucky I am to have a mother who cares so much. Friends who've lost their mothers tell me how difficult it is when they realize that they'll never again find another person so totally focused on their well-being.

The most devoted friend, lover, or even husband would never call you in a panic to warn you of the dangers of nylon-crotched panties. And they wouldn't *dream* of advising you to alternate which side you wear your purse on so your shoulders don't get uneven.

As you flip through this book, smiling and maybe even laughing your *tuchas* off at my existence under Mom's Rule, a few questions may come up.

First, you may wonder why my mother calls me "Amila" (pronounced AY-muh-luh) when my name is actually Amy. The answer is that, as a classic Jewish mother, my mom follows the tradition of adding an "ila" to my name as a term of endearment. (This is probably why you rarely hear of a Jewish girl named something like "Lola"—her mother would then have to call her Lola-ila, which doesn't roll very smoothly off the tongue.) You'll also find that my mother sometimes calls me *"mamascheinz,"* which literally translates to "sweet mother" but can be used affectionately for anyone female, much as Spanish-speaking people might use *"mamacita."* And here and there, my mother uses some other Yiddish phrases, which are explained in the glossary at the end of this book.

At some point you may also wonder, "Where *is* Amy while her mother's calling and chatting up a storm with her machine? Is she sitting there screening or what?"

The answer is "or what."

For the past several years, my answering machine has had a light on but nobody home, due mostly to my insane hours as a creative director at a New York ad agency. On top of that, I began doing stand-up comedy, which is how *Amy's Answering Machine* came about.

When I first played my mother's messages on stage and saw how much audiences loved her (Why is it always easier to see the humor in someone *else's* mother?), I decided to produce my own CD and market it through my Website.

Then, when the success of the CD showed just *how many* people related to and were entertained by my struggles with Mom, I was offered the opportunity to write this book.

If your own mother drives you crazy, I hope my book will help you find some comfort in knowing you're not alone.

If you *are* a mother who drives your kids crazy, maybe it will help you see yourself in a new light and take steps toward rehabilitation.

And if your mother is no longer with you and you actually *miss* the infuriating advice, questions, and comments, I hope my mother's messages will bring you more laughter than tears.

Wishing only health, happiness, and love for you, your mother, and mine,

Amy Borkowsky

HOW COME EVERY TIME I HIT "PLAY" ON MY ANSWERING MACHINE MY MOTHER IS PUSHING *MY* BUTTONS?

· · · · · · · · · · · · · · · · · · ·

I have a radio that gives weather forecasts every few minutes, and cable TV with a channel devoted entirely to the weather. So why does my mother always feel compelled to call me up with a weather report?

"Amila? I hope you're on your way home. I just heard on the weather, there's a big storm headed for New York and they're expecting four to six inches in the city, with accumulations of up to a foot in the outlying areas. So if I were you, I wouldn't go *shlepping* to any outlying areas. On the weather map, all over New York, they had snowflakes the size of bagels. So if you have to go out, make sure you bundle up. And wrap a scarf around your face to protect it, 'cause y'know, there was that man who climbed Mount Everest and lost his entire nose. Okay, honey? I love you. Bye."

Somehow I just don't see anywhere I would *shlep* to as being quite parallel to climbing Mt. Everest.

"Our guest today is Amila Borkowsky, the first woman ever to reach the summit of Macy's department store. So, Amila, what was it like up there?"

"Words just can't describe it. The view of Linens and Housewares was *breathtaking.*"

"Now the question everyone wants to know is, what did you buy?"

"Nothing. By the time I got there, they didn't have the one item I really needed."

"What was that?"

"A new nose."

Amila ignores Mom's advice to protect
her face with a scarf and pays the price.

To my mother, any story she hears on the news is directly related to my well-being.

"Hi, Amila. I was watching the news, and I heard about that little girl who was alone in an apartment for nine days without food, and it made me think of you. Honey, please, be sure you have what to eat in the fridge, 'cause last time you came to visit, you looked like Olive Oyl. Okay, honey, bye-bye."

Like a lot of women, my mother has a distorted body image. Only it's my body she's distorting. I really believe I could gain eighty pounds and would still look too thin to my mother.

And how could she see any connection between me and the "little girl"? I've been alone in my apartment for nine *years* with an empty fridge and I'm still here.

That's because I'm a grown-up and can easily go to salad bars, restaurants, or order a pizza.

Really, the only time my empty fridge has been a major problem is if, say, a guy comes over after a date: "Boy, I'm starving, Amila. What do you have in the fridge?"

"Let's see, Barry. Can I offer you some duck sauce? Or . . . how would you like a nice stick of butter?"

Of course, I realize all my mother's irritating reminders about having enough food do come from a very loving place. All she wants is to see me thrive.

And I know that when I appear on television, my mother is sitting at home, just beaming with joy.

Mainly because TV adds ten pounds.

Amila offers her date a little something from the fridge.

So why does my mother always have to repeat herself?

"Hi, Amila. I still haven't heard whether or not you got the package I sent you. It's a large padded envelope that says 'Priority Mail'—'cause you're a priority honey. So go and check downstairs and see if there's a large, padded Priority Mail envelope. Okay? It's not a regular envelope—it's a Priority one that's large and padded. All right, so call me as soon as you get the package. But it's not really a package per se, so keep your eyes open for a large padded Priority Mail envelope. All right, *mamascheinz,* bye-bye."

While a mother's constant repetition is annoying enough in face-to-face conversation, it's even more unnecessary on an answering machine. If I didn't catch something my mother said, couldn't I just hit "rewind" and replay it?

While a mother's constant repetition is annoying enough in face-to-face conversation, it's even more unnecessary on an answering machine. If I didn't catch something my mother said, couldn't I just hit "rewind" and replay it?

Note to mothers: Now you know how *we* feel.

I imagine my mother must have some measure of peace knowing I live in New York, New York—a city that automatically repeats itself.

Even in the simplest things I enjoy—like listening to music—my mother will find some element of danger.

"Hello, Amila. Yeah, I don't know if you heard the latest on the portable stereos, but they're saying that the foam earpiece on the headphones is a prime breeding ground for bacteria. So if you still insist on walking around with the headphones on, you may wanna take an antibiotic. Okay, hon? Talk to you soon. Bye."

First of all, I only owned a portable stereo for three weeks out of my life. It was actually just a mini-FM receiver that was so "mini" I lost it, probably in the seat cushions of a taxi. But because my mother happened to see me wearing the Bacteria Breeder on one particular visit, she naturally assumed it was as much a part of what I wore every day as, say, deodorant.

This is what happens when your parents live out of town and you don't see them often. They assume even random behavior observed on a single visit is habitual. One time, while I was visiting my father, we stopped into a diner and, for a little change of pace, I ordered a pork chop. This was one of only three pork chops I'd eaten in my entire life, but from that day on, I became known to my father as The Daughter Who Eats Pork Chops.

But back to my mother. Let's suppose, for a moment, that I *was* a habitual headphone wearer. Where would I find a doctor *willing* to write me an antibiotic prescription?

"Doctor, you've gotta help me. I have Headphones."

"Well, Amila, I'm sorry, but the only thing we could do for you at this point would involve surgery."

"Surgery?"

"Yes. Basically, we'd have no choice but to remove your headphones."

"*Please*, couldn't you just write me a prescription?"

"Well, if you still insist on walking around and listening to music, I suppose I could write you a prescription. For a boombox."

Not only does my mother use my answering machine to control my life, she also uses it to control the machine itself.

"Hi, Amila. I don't like the new message you have on your machine. You're letting the whole world know that you're not at home. It'd be better to say something like, 'Thank you for calling but I am presently indisposed.' That way they'll just think you're on the toilet. Or on second thought, don't even say 'I.' Just say, 'Nobody can get to the phone right now because we are presently indisposed.' Okay, honey? Bye-bye."

"Amila, it's me again. Where are you? You must be downstairs with the laundry. I know I'm using up your tape, but it just occurred to me, if you use the word 'we,' a guy you're interested in might think you're married. So it'd probably be better not to use any pronouns. You could just say something like, 'Thank you for calling. Leave a message.' And you don't have to tell them what to do after the beep, 'cause by now, anyone who doesn't know that is a total *shmegegge*. Okay, I know I'm using up your tape, honey. Call me back. Bye-bye."

• •

Whenever I change my outgoing message, my mother becomes the Roger Ebert of answering machines, critiquing my "work" as if it were a major motion picture. Her comments have ranged from "It sounds like you're in a well" to "The music in the background sounds like a brothel."

I could see her having her own show:

"Good evening. I'm Mrs. Borkowsky with a review of Amila's latest outgoing message. I must admit, my expectations were quite high, since my Amila generally has a very good head on her shoulders. However, I nearly *plotzed* when I heard her say, 'Hello, you've reached five-five-five-three-two-three-one.' What if some lunatic dialed her number at random? Why remind him of what number he called so he can go and do it again? Not to compare her to my other daughter— since, of course, I love them both equally—but her sister Judy used much better judgment when she stuck with the computerized voice that came with the machine. It says, simply, 'Please leave a message.' This is one case where less really is more. So, while I applaud Amila for her great pronunciation of the numbers—her delivery of 'three-two-three-one' was very convincing—I'm going to have to give her latest outgoing message one-and-a-half matzoh balls."

A lot of Internet sites are advertising that they can personalize their home page so you get the news stories that apply to you. What's the big deal? My mother's been providing this service for years.

"Amila? I don't think you went to bed yet, but maybe you're in the tub. I wanted to know if you by any chance happened to catch the story on the new squirting scam. Apparently, the way it works is, you'll be walking along the street and, unbeknownst to you, some guy or maybe a woman will squirt you from behind with a bottle of ketchup. Then, someone else who's in cahoots with that person will say, 'Excuse me, Miss, but there's some ketchup on your sweater.' And then, just as you go to wipe it, they grab your bag and that's the end of that. I just figured I'd mention it, so if somebody tries to point out any ketchup on you, you'll be wise to it, and you can just say something like, 'I'm well aware of the ketchup—

in fact, it matches my pants that have a big blob of relish.' Then as they're looking down at your pants, you can make a quick getaway and go report it to the police. All right, I hope you're doing good, and I'll talk to you tomorrow. Bye-bye."

• •

In a world where innocent people are being randomly attacked with guns, knives, and AIDS-filled syringes, I find it hard to lose even a millisecond of sleep worrying that someone's going to come after me with a bottle of ketchup.

I mean, if this were *really* a threat, wouldn't people be lobbying for ketchup control?

Wouldn't they install ketchup detectors at the airports?

And anyway, it usually takes me forty-five minutes of smacking a ketchup bottle to get one drop out; if some stranger can manage to squirt it out fast enough to catch me off guard, that's not a crime.

That's an accomplishment.

Now, if they took my wallet in the process, well, that *would* make me mad.

Yeah, the more I think about it, I'm *glad* my mother warned me.

I'm not going to stand by, passively, helplessly waiting to be The Next Victim. I'm going to Take Action and Arm Myself.

With a jar of mayo.

Amila fights off the notorious ketchup-wielding bandit.

My mother still doesn't seem to realize that I'm capable of taking care of some really very basic needs.

"Hi, Amila. It's me, honey. If you haven't already left to go to the motor vehicle bureau, keep in mind that the wait is very long. So before you get in line, you may wanna empty your bladder. All right, honey, that's all for now. Bye-bye."

What gets me, first of all, is that she thinks I wouldn't already *know* there'd be a wait at the DMV—as if I'm under the impression that the DMV in Manhattan gives *instant* service. Like maybe I'm figuring I'll go over there and the smiling DMV clerk will meet me *at the door:*

"Here's your license, Ma'am, and remember: 'DMV' stands for Done in a *Moment's* Visit!"

And even if the line *were* longer than expected and I felt like I could burst a water main, when I got to the organ donor check box, I'd just write in, 'Take my bladder. *Now.*'

Mom Years

Mothers experience time in a totally different way when it comes to their kids. Recently, I was visiting my mother, when she casually suggested, "Why don't you put your hair up in a bun like you wear it sometimes."

"What do you mean 'sometimes'—I *never* wear my hair in a bun."

"Yes, you do—you know, how you pull it up off your face and wrap it with bobby pins?"

"Mom, I haven't worn a bun since I was seventeen!"

"So what are you arguing with me for? You just said so yourself. That's how you sometimes wear your hair."

The truth is, to a mother, even something you did twenty years ago seems like a-bat-of-an-eyelash ago. All mothers are programmed to calculate time in Mom Years, which are a lot like dog years, though the mathematical conversion process is somewhat simpler. To convert normal years into Mom Years, divide the number of years by itself, then subtract 364 days.

For example, if your first day of kindergarten was twenty years ago, your calculations would be as follows: 20÷20 = 1 year; 1 year − 364 days = Just Yesterday.

Why is it that my mother always seems to examine me with a magnifying glass?

"Hello, Amila. I guess you must be out shopping. I meant to mention something when you were here, but since I didn't get a chance, I figured I'd just leave it on your machine. I don't know if you're aware of it, but when I was taking the pictures and you smiled, I noticed that one of your eyes—I think it was the left one—was staying partially shut, like about a fifth to maybe a third of the way. It looked sort of like a person who's all liquored up trying to wink. You may wanna ask an ophthalmologist about it. And in the meantime, just try and be aware of it, 'cause someone could interpret the wink as body language for an invitation to *shtup*. Okay, I'll talk to you soon. Bye-bye."

All mothers believe they're blessed with superior vision when it comes to looking at their children. Much as a dog can hear sounds not audible to humans, mothers believe they can see things not visible to the ordinary eye.

Every time I visit my mother, the first thing she does is give me a really loving hug, as she beams with maternal pride, and says, "Oy, *mamascheinz,* you look beautiful."

Then suddenly, as she shifts her gaze to my right cheek, the maternal pride gives way to a look of grave concern, as if Death itself were knocking at the door. "That mole on your cheek—did it get bigger? It looks bigger."

For the record, that spot on my cheek that my mother *used* to call a "beauty mark" has been the same size for as long as I can remember.

The mole comment is always followed by another hug and comment about my exceptional beauty, after which she pulls away slightly to examine The Entire Daughter from head to toe. "You look too thin, like you lost weight. Did you lose weight?"

I once figured out that, based on the minimal weight loss that would be noticeable to the human eye, if I *had* lost weight every time she said that, I should now weigh just over twelve pounds.

Amila arrives at Mom's house for her semi-annual inspection.

The way my mother talks to me sometimes, she apparently must think I'm some kind of an idiot.

"Hi, Amila. I was just thinking that for your friend Susan's housewarming, you might wanna get her a gift certificate from Crate and Barrel. That's C-R-A-T-E and barrel—B-A-R-R-E-L. You can remember it because it rhymes with Sandy's in-laws, Nate and Carol. All right, honey, bye-bye."

I think my mother's passion for spelling stems from a desire to make sure that I absolutely, positively, fully understand the critically important things she has to tell me.

Pretty ironic, considering there was a time when she'd spell to make sure I *didn't* understand—as in, "Doctor, I'm very concerned about my Amila because she eats like an s-p-a-r-r-o-w."

We did get into a heated debate over how to spell her nickname for me, "Amila." (Remember, until *Amy's Answering Machine* came about, there really was no reason for me to ever *write* the name.)

Here were all the candidates for spellings, along with the reasons why they were rejected.

Amilah: My mother was lobbying for this spelling, because she thought the final "h" put me in a prime position to "burst onto the scene as a Jewish Oprah." She argued that the final "h" added a touch of class—until I reminded her of "feh" and "pish," Yiddish words that roughly translate to "yuck" and "to relieve one's bladder."

Amyla: This was my first choice. I thought that the "y" in the middle added a hipness and a downtown edge. My mother, always the Spelling Queen, accurately pointed out, "Look, if you wanna be hip, just remember that 'hip' has an 'i' in the middle, not a 'y.' Okay, chalk one up for Mom.

Amela: I strongly vetoed this one because I felt then, and still do, that it comes dangerously close to "Amelia" and could cause confusion. Thankfully, Mom agreed: "It reminds me too much of Amelia Earhart, which is no good—remember, that girl got on an airplane and her mother never saw her again."

So, by process of elimination, I'm writing to you now as the artist alternately known as "Amila."

I can't seem to make my mother understand that there are some parts of my life that are just not a mother's business.

·  · · · · · · · · · · · · · · · · · ·

"Hi, Amila. I had something on my mind that I wanted to tell you, but I don't want you to get mad at me. I just wanna make sure if you get involved with someone, that you don't use lambskin condoms. Because if you're worried about AIDS, using lambskin is the same as if the guy had a totally naked *shmekel*. And they used to make graduation certificates out of sheepskin. So before you do anything foolish, you may wanna ask yourself, How safe would I feel with his *shmekel* wrapped in a diploma? Okay, that's my two cents for now. I'll talk to you later."

· ·

This is the reason I always keep the volume down on my machine when I have a guy over. If a boyfriend heard something like this, his *shmekel* would immediately shrink down to nothing.

And really, isn't she *reaching* with the condom/diploma analogy?

If they really *were* that similar, why would there be all that controversy over giving out condoms in the schools? In fact, at graduation, principals could hand each graduate a condom *instead of* a diploma.

How proud the parents would be, as the band played "Pomp and Circumstance" and the PA system blared, "And now, receiving his Bachelor of Science with Lubrication, Michael Adam Klein."

Why a Mother
Is Better Than a Guy

As a single woman on the dating scene, I have to appreciate one thing about mothers. When a mother says, "I'll call you," you *know* she's going to call.

When a mother *doesn't* say, "I'll call you," you *know* she's going to call.

And when a mother says, "I'm *never, ever, ever* calling you again," well, only then do you know for sure that you won't hear from her again.

Until tomorrow.

A mother will never leave you in a position where you have to call your girlfriends and ask, "I saw her on Saturday, and it's Wednesday already. If I don't hear from her by tomorrow, do you think it's okay for me to call?"

Of course, my advice is, if you *do* find a guy who calls as often as your mother, whatever you do, hold onto him and *don't let him go*.

Until the police can get there and arrest him for stalking.

Any time I tell my mother an idea for something I'm excited to do, she will immediately jump to point out the negatives.

"Yeah, it's me Amila. I was thinking, I don't know if it's such a good idea for you to get a cat. They get hairs all over everything and they *pish* on the rug. And then all of a sudden, you have vet bills. A lady by me paid twice as much to fix her cat's paw as she did for her own thyroid. And what if you finally found a nice guy and he was allergic? Yeah, you'll tell him, 'Love me, love my cat,' and he'll say, 'Fine. I don't love you, and your cat can kiss my *tuchas*.' So think about it, honey, okay? All right. Bye."

Now her first point is, basically, that I shouldn't get a cat because it might put a crimp in my housekeeping.

Well, by that logic, I shouldn't get a husband, either, since I hear they leave toilet seats up and socks on the floor.

To reassure myself that I could overcome my mother's Cat-owning Concerns, I consulted prominent New York veterinarian Lawrence A. Putter. Dr. Putter's opinion, based on over a decade of caring for domesticated animals, was as follows: "If the cat sheds, you'll just vacuum."

Further, Dr. Putter assured me that a healthy young cat "will not, under most circumstances, exhibit any random pishing."

Now if I *did* finally meet a nice guy who was allergic—well, my mother's right on that one— that would be a problem.

I'd feel terrible doing it, but I guess I'd just have to take an ad out in the paper:

Single woman with friendly, beautiful, housebroken Tabby has finally met nice guy who's allergic. Seeking loving person, with room in her heart and her apartment, to take the guy.

Every year on my birthday, my mother calls with birthday wishes. One year, it had a special twist.

(Singing)   "Happy birthday to you,
                  Happy birthday to you,
                  Happy birthday dear Amila,
                  Happy birthday to you.
                  How old are you now,
                  How old are you now,
                  Better hurry and find a husband,
                  Before your ovaries shut down.

All right, that's just a little creativity for my birthday girl. I love you sweetie."

I wish someone would please explain to me how come in *all* other aspects of life, my mother sees me as being practically a toddler, but when it comes to settling down and having kids, suddenly I'm over the hill?

And what if my ovaries really *were* ready to shut down? What does she expect me to do—get on a loudspeaker and make an announcement?

"Attention all single males. Amy's ovaries will be closing in fifteen minutes. Please decide if Amy is your final selection, and proceed with your gonads to the checkout."

Mom sends Amila a birthday cake with a very special ingredient.

Mom's Favorite Sport

The answering machine is the arena where a mother avidly engages in her favorite sport, Guessing Where My Child Is. She believes herself to be The Person on the Planet Who Knows You Best, and proudly enjoys displaying this knowledge on your machine.

The only problem is, she's always wrong.

In my mother's case, her most frequent guesses include, "I assume you went to brunch with Alison," "Maybe you're in the tub," and "You must be downstairs doing laundry."

The reality is, most mothers have no clue as to how you *really* live your life, but apparently the guessing process is in itself rewarding enough, since all my friends tell me their mothers do the same thing.

I'm surprised no network has picked up on this trend yet and launched a game show version:

"Good evening and welcome to *Guess Where My Child Is*, the show where mothers flaunt their knowledge of their daughters' whereabouts for cash jackpots and fabulous prizes! Our first contestant is Amila's Mom, who'll be competing against our returning champion, Estelle Greene—mother of Lori—who last week correctly guessed that Lori was at the

Miss Nails salon getting a wrap and tips. Okay, Amila's mom, you know the way it works, so pick up your telephone, and let's go *dialing for daughters!*

"All right, it's ringing . . . still ringing . . . okay, we got her machine. So, Amila's mom, for fifty thousand dollars in cash and a chance to advance to the bonus round, where is Amila?"

"Well, let's see, it's Thursday night and it's after eight-thirty . . . she's normally home at this hour . . . and she has to work on Friday, so if she's not there . . . my guess would be . . . Jack, this is a tough one, but I'm gonna guess Amila's in the Roosevelt Hospital emergency room."

At this point, a collective gasp would erupt from the audience.

"That's quite a leap. Are you sure that's your guess?"

"I think so. Yeah, I'll stick with that."

"Okay, well, Vera the Verifier has Roosevelt Hospital on the other line, and they've just informed us that nobody by the name of Amila Borkowsky has been admitted to the ER this evening. I'm *so sorry,* but thank you for playing."

"Oh, don't be sorry, Jack. I had a feeling I was wrong. When the audience gasped, I knew I shoulda gone with my other answer."

"What was that?"

"The Mount Sinai emergency room."

I'm such a *huge* part of my mother's life that even a total stranger can pick up on it.

"Yeah, hello, Amila. It's me. You remember that program I love to watch with the live psychics? Well, I called up this one gal named Natasha for a reading, and she was absolutely marvelous. The first thing she asked right off the bat was if I had a daughter whose name contained a vowel. She said like either an 'a' or an 'e.' And she saw you romantically involved with a very nice guy who may be going bald, but you shouldn't reject him because of that, because she said he'll bring you much happiness, and he can always buy a toupee. So that should be some good news for you, honey. Call me when you get in. Love you. Bye."

My mother became so enamored with her favorite show that she would actually call up the production staff just to chat—and, of course, to give them advice.

"Hi, Amila. I just got off the phone with Ricardo, the director of that psychic show. I called him up on their studio line to give him a few pointers. I told him, first of all, that their backdrop looks like some kid went and splashed paint on it. And I told him the fill-in psychic is not very telegenic. She looks like a female George Washington. Well, I was surprised, 'cause he was very receptive. I think he got a kick out of me. He said I should let him know when I'll be coming to New York and said I could come by the studio and meet everybody. So I'll have to come and take you with me to meet my psychic buddies, okay? All right. We'll talk later."

Mom was very excited. For her, an invitation to the Psychics' Studio was like an invitation to the White House.

Frankly, I was looking forward to it myself. I would love to be able to shake the hand of the woman who *intuitively knew* that my name contained a vowel. How proud she would be to hear my mother call me, "Amila," a name that contains *three* vowels, *two* of which are "a"—*exactly* the letter that she had predicted!

And there was so much I wanted to ask her about Mr. Balding. Where would I meet him? Would he be intelligent? Successful? Allergic to cats? Would he necessarily be a toupee candidate, or might he be *destined for hair plugs?*

I'm sorry to report that this story has a very tragic ending. Just days after Ricardo, The Director of That Psychic Show, extended his gracious offer for my mother to visit, the show went off the air. It was finished. Kaput. Banished forever to psychic show heaven. My mother *tried in vain* to call Ricardo, but apparently the number had been disconnected.

For weeks she went flipping through channels, hoping against hope that maybe the show had just switched stations, but Natasha and Ricardo were nowhere to be found.

I told her, "Don't worry, Mom. I'm sure someday they'll resurface. I'm picking up a strong feeling about it. I see them either on a station on the West Coast beginning with a 'K' or possibly an East Coast channel with a 'W.' "

With all the joy the psychics brought her, I hope I'm right.

If it were up to my mother, to this day she would still dress me.

"Hi, Amila. It's me. Y'know the red terry robe you wore when I came to visit—it's like a ruby red with a belt? Do you still wear that or did you throw it out? I just wanna tell you that if you take out the garbage or run to the mailbox, you may wanna put on something else, because my friend Eileen's grandson said that red is a gang color. Okay, Sweetie-pie? Talk to you later."

Now, what are the odds that two violent street gangs are going to decide to have it out on the twelfth floor of a Murray Hill doorman building, at the *exact* moment that I'm carrying out a bag of trash, totally oblivious to the Crips and the Bloods lining the hallway?

They'll be yelling, "Don't go after Julio—*he's* not the leader."

"It's . . . it's the Jewish girl in the bathrobe!"

Amila takes out the trash in her ruby red robe.

Having a mother like mine is like having a consumer advocate who's way too consumed with me.

"Amila, it's me. I had a thought. Just 'cause the store has such a crazy return policy is no reason you should suffer. If I were you, I would just explain that you were visiting your mother so you couldn't get there within thirty days. What did they expect you to do? They think you're gonna call me up, 'Mom, I can't come for Thanksgiving because I have to bring back some pants?' And don't let them talk you into any merchandise credit. The credit slip will sit in your wallet 'til it's all shredded and crumpled, and you won't know whether you should use it to buy pants or blow your nose. So go ahead, *mamascheinz,* plead your case with the manager and let me know how it works out, okay. Okay, honey, bye-bye."

Here's what happened. I had purchased a pair of blue velvet pants at the one-day sale of a major New York department store whose return period for sale items is thirty days. On day twenty-eight, I went out-of-town to visit Mom and didn't get back to the store until five days *after* the return period.

So the bottom line is, it was *my fault* that I missed the deadline.

Nevertheless, this monthlong return window fits what my mother seems to think is the definition of a Crazy Policy under New York State law: Any policy that challenges, competes with, or otherwise fails to meet the needs of Amila.

At the very least, for taking my side and always looking out for my best interest, I have to give her credit.

But it won't be on a piece of paper, or it'll get all shredded and crumpled and, well, you know the rest.

A Hit Series About Moms

With all the drama that Mom brings to my daily life, it got me thinking: Why not have a new series about an emergency room that specializes in the life-and-death concerns of mothers. The show would be called, M-o-t-h-*ER*. Instead of George Clooney, it'd star Rosemary Clooney, handling such catastrophic events as:

◆   a mother who desperately tries to save her son from a downward spiral of self-destruction that culminates in his going swimming *less than twenty-five minutes after eating*

◆   a mother on the verge of becoming *a broken woman* when she learns that her daughter, barely thirty, *goes outside with a damp head.* (This episode might be too dark and depressing to have prime-time network appeal, but could perhaps be toned down by having the daughter go out with her jacket unzipped.)

◆   a mother who enlists the aid of specialists in the m-o-t-h-*ER* when she is unable to contact her daughter to inform her that carrying cash in a backpack is *inviting theft.* Will the crack team in the m-o-t-h-*ER* be able to locate the daughter and convince her to *tuck the bills into her bra?*

My mother is a very honest person, and when she sees dishonesty in her world, it upsets her, and she calls me to vent.

"Hi, Amila, it's me honey. I'm so annoyed I could bust. I just saw Barbara downstairs and she was bragging how a friend of hers brought her some real New York rye bread, and Amila, I swear there's no way that's New York rye bread because as God is my witness, I know that bread came from New Jersey. So finally I confronted her about it because evidently she forgot that she told me her friend is from New Jersey. And you know what she finally admitted? It was baked in New York, but the dough was from Paramus. Well I got the name of the bakery and you know what else I found out? The caraway seeds are from Hartford, Connecticut. Don't call me back tonight, honey, because this whole thing has me too upset. All right, I'll talk to you tomorrow. Bye-bye."

Gosh, I actually *wanted* to call her back. This was a Very Serious Matter, and I had questions. Lots of them.

Like, what about the dough *ingredients?* Where was the yeast from? The flour? The water?

For a legal perspective on the issue, I consulted attorney Marvin Katzman of the esteemed law firm Katzman and Weiss. Mr. Katzman was reluctant to offer a definitive opinion on what he admitted was a "gray area," but said: "The closest precedent is a ruling which states that for sparkling wine to be called 'champagne,' it must not just be bottled in the Champagne region of France but made with grapes from the Champagne region."

Well, then, shouldn't the same logic hold for a loaf of bread?

Further complicating the matter is that there's a town in New York that's named "Rye," so even if every molecule in the bread hailed from the state of New York, could you legally call it "rye" if it were not from the town of Rye, but from, say, Great Neck? Would it then be more accurate to call it New York Great Neck bread?

All sarcasm aside, I applaud my mother for standing up for what is Fair and Just. And she has equally high moral values for issues that go way beyond the scope of a loaf of bread.

She also applies these principles to cake.

Last time Mom was visiting, we had dinner in a restaurant at the South Street Seaport, where she ordered the Triple Chocolate Cake, "a decadent dessert made with three kinds of chocolate." Just a couple of forkfuls into the cake, my mother summoned the waiter:

"Excuse, me, sir, but this is *not* triple chocolate cake."

"Uh, yes it is, Ma'am."

"Then how come I only taste two kinds of chocolate?"

"Would you like me to bring you something else?"

"Yes."

"Okay, what would you like?"

"A side order of the third chocolate."

Day nine of the New York Rye trial.

One of my advertising clients was based in Washington, DC. This is the message I got on my machine after I told my mother I might stay over after my Friday meeting and do some sightseeing.

"Hello, Amila. It's me, honey. I know you're all excited about your trip to Washington, but I wanna remind you that it's very windy by the Washington Monument, so you may wanna take along a hat. And if you happen to take a tour of the White House, whatever you do, don't let them leave you alone with the president. So call me before you leave. Bye-bye."

What was my mother thinking? Just how likely did she think it was that President Clinton would be trolling the lines of White House tourists just as *I* happen to be working my way through, and that, of the *hundreds* of women in the line, he'd single *me* out to hit on:

"Excuse me. I couldn't help but notice you on the

tour line. When the guide said, 'To your right is the blue room,' I was enchanted by the way you craned your neck."

"Oh, thank you."

"Look, I don't normally do this, but, uh, I was wondering if you might like to join me for a cup of coffee. Or maybe a cigar."

"I'm sorry, Mr. President, but before I left, my mother told me to make sure I have a hat—and she really stressed that I shouldn't be alone with you."

"No problem. I totally understand."

"You do?"

"Sure. So I'll bring along some interns."

"Gee, I don't know."

"Then how about a little ride in the backseat of my limo?"

"It's a tempting offer, but I just wouldn't feel right disobeying my mother."

"I can respect that."

"You can?"

"Of course. I won't mind at all if you wear a hat."

Backup arrives to protect Amila from presidential advances.

When I go to the airport, I'm happy if all my stuff fits in my suitcase and I get to my plane on time. My mother worries about other things that in *a million years* would never have entered my mind.

"Yeah, Amila. It's me. I meant to tell you, so you don't set off the metal detector at the airport, make sure that when you leave the house, you don't wear an underwire bra. A lady on the bus said it happened to a woman she knew, and she claims they frisked her for four hours. Even if she's exaggerating and it was only two, that's a long time to have a stranger surveying your land. So, just for one day, you may even wanna consider going braless. So have a wonderful trip, and call me when you get to the hotel, okay? Love you. Bye."

First off, let me just say that I'm flattered my mother thinks I have enough "land" to "survey" that I might actually need the support of an underwire bra. This is a rare example of her acknowledging me as a fully developed adult woman.

I'll never forget how embarrassed I felt when I was in junior high and overheard my mother talking to a friend of hers on the phone; apparently, the friend must have asked about my newly developing figure, because all I heard was my mother's response: "Well, let's just say there are, uh, how should I put it—two mosquito bites."

I probably need some calamine lotion, 'cause those bites are still there.

I can't recall ever taking a trip and *not* getting a phone call from my mother confirming my safe arrival home and questioning me about the flight experience. However, this questionnaire rarely comes in the form of a message; I may hear several hang-ups on my machine, but this all-important flight follow-up is always conducted live, voice-to-voice.

●●●◀

Mom's Flight Satisfaction Survey

Q1. How was your flight?

Q2. Did they give you anything to eat?

(If "no") Oy, you must be starving. Are you starving?

(If "yes") What did they give you?

(If meal contains less than three thousand calories) Oy, you must be starving. Are you starving?

Q3. Did you sit next to anyone interesting?

(If male) Was he single?

(If "yes") Did he take your number?

(If "no") Did you get his card?

Q4. So what time did you get in?

(If after 6:00 P.M.) Oy, you must be exhausted. Are you exhausted?

(If "no") See? You don't even *realize* you're so exhausted 'cause you're overtired.

The TV only feeds my mother's already obsessive concern over my safety.

"Yeah, hello, Amila. They just said on TV, 'It's ten P.M., do you know where your children are?' and I'm thinking, I don't know, so I figured I'd call you, *mamascheinz.* You must be in the bathroom or something. Give me a buzz when you're done, okay? All right, bye-bye."

"Amila? It's five to eleven and I know you have work tomorrow. I'm getting a little worried. Call me when you get this message, honey. Okay, bye-bye."

This message was followed by four separate messages— from my friends Michael, Sherry, Alison, and Leslie— each saying that my mother had called them looking for me. But it didn't end there.

"Hi, Amy. Yeah, it's Andrew. I just got a call from your mom about ten minutes ago, and she wanted to know if you were spending the night at my house. I told her we broke up four years ago."

"Hello, Miss Borkowsky? Hi, I'm calling from NYU Hospital. Someone called here claiming to be your mother and wanting to know if you'd been admitted."

So where *was* I, you ask? Passed out drunk at some wild sex orgy? Abducted by a group of militant guerrillas?

Actually, I was somewhere far more shocking.

In my own bed. Sound asleep. Since *nine-thirty*.

Exhausted from too many late nights at the ad agency, I'd conked out early and had just turned my ringer off. When I woke up the next morning, I was *so* mad.

I could only imagine who she would have called next . . .

(Ring, ring.)

"Good morning. National Dairy Board."

"Uh, yes, I'd like to find out how I can get my child's picture on a milk carton."

"How long has the child been missing?"

"A *very* long time. I'd say well over ninety minutes."

"Okay, Ma'am, is this a boy or a girl?"

"It's a girl—my Amila."

"And what was she wearing when she disappeared?"

"Let's see . . . she probably had on a silk blouse with maybe a dark blazer, a matching skirt, and a pair of pumps."

"Was she playing dress up?"

"No. But she mentioned today she had to go see a new client."

"Ma'am, how old is your Amila?"

"Thirty-four and three quarters."

*After unplugging her phone, Amila awakens
to learn that Mom has put out an APB.*

A mother has no place getting involved in my career.

················· **B E E P** ·····················

"Oh, hi, Amila. Your machine picked up so fast this time—your message tape must be full. Yeah, I was thinking, I don't like the fact that that headhunter is keeping your portfolio tied up for so long. It's unprofessional, and she's keeping you from pursuing your livelihood, which is really unfair. If she doesn't get it back to you by Friday, do you think maybe *I* should call? If you think that might get some results, leave me her number, and I'll do it tomorrow morning before I go to the podiatrist, okay? Okay, bye-bye."

·····································

Now *this* would present me as the take-charge woman on her way to top management:

"Hi, I'm calling on behalf of Amy Borkowsky who's seeking a position as Executive Vice President and Creative Director."

"Are you her assistant?"

"No, I'm her mother."

Even after I told her that her stepping in would send the wrong message, she insisted, "The only statement it's making is that you have a mother who cares about your success."

Okay, she has always been *very* supportive of my career, but she has to learn where to draw the line.

It would not surprise me in the least to see my mother leading the charge to organize a Take Your Mothers to Work Day.

Why does my mother think it's necessary to go to the ends of the Earth to find me a date?

"Hi, Amila. I don't know if you saw, this week in *People* magazine, there's an article on a single, Jewish guy who owns a restaurant in Fairbanks, Alaska, and he's now in New York looking for a wife. He looks *eppes* like a young Jackie Mason. Anyway, you know my friend Muriel saw the same article, so you better hurry up and contact him before her daughter does. So call me tonight and I'll give you the information. At least if he's from Alaska, you figure he knows how to pick out a fresh salmon. Oh, and in case you get along and you go to visit his family, you may wanna think about getting a Polartec jacket. Well, I should be up until at least eleven so call me."

I'm impressed that she would actually consider shipping me off to the farthest, most frigid place on the planet. I did happen to see the article and, if I remember correctly, the chosen bride would have been required to relocate *permanently* to Alaska. Obviously, she missed this critical fact, because I don't think she would have found the guy's natural salmon-picking ability enough of a plus to outweigh it.

Or maybe she just got caught up in some romanticized notion of me and The Young Jackie Mason in a sprawling, ranch-style igloo. I could see it myself: After a long day of toiling at His Own Restaurant, Young Jackie would come bounding up our driveway with a kettle full of fresh salmon and I'd greet him at the door in a Polartec teddy. Then we'd make love until the sun came up. Which, in Alaska, could be three months.

That's the fantasy. The reality? I'm sure it'd be only a matter of time—like twelve minutes—before I'd be deluged with messages like "They say colds are passed by nasal viruses, so don't let any Alaskans talk you into rubbing noses" or "If you happen to get hit on the head by a falling icicle, remember to *put ice on it.*"

*Realizing she's The One, the Alaska Bachelor
takes Amila shopping for a flawless salmon.*

Call Prying

The feature known colloquially as "call waiting" is more accurately referred to as "call prying," because it obviously was designed by a mother as an invitation to pry for details on her child's social life.

Here's how it works: Whenever I'm talking to my mother and another call clicks in, she always asks, "So who was that?"

"Just a friend."

"Which friend?"

"Mom, it's a personal call. I'd rather not say."

"Was it a guy?"

"Okay, fine, it was a guy. Let's just leave it at that."

The goal with the call prying interrogation is to communicate to your mother that you *do* have a social life but not to give her too much information that could lead to further questioning.

And anyway, I just don't think it's necessary to give my mother every little detail of all the guys who call me.

Especially when most of them are selling magazines and time-shares.

I live in the same neighborhood as the United Nations, and whenever countries gather to work toward peace, I have *anything but* from my mother.

"Hi, Amila. I just heard about that meeting at the U.N., and I hear the whole area is a madhouse. If you look out your window, you may even be able to see *eppes* some kind of demonstration. It sounds like they're making all kinds of crazy threats, so until it all subsides, I would really recommend that you stay inside and maybe order dinner in. Just for tonight, if you can avoid it, I wouldn't order, like, Chinese or even, say, Indian 'cause with all that's going on, you don't know who might have it in for that particular country and what they could stick in the food. So you may wanna play it safe and order from a diner. All right, Amila, give me a call."

Hypothetically, if I give my mother the benefit of a *huge* doubt and embrace her international food fight theory, a diner really wouldn't be any safer than an ethnic restaurant; a good percentage of the diners in New York are owned by Greeks, which means the diner food could be tainted by any country that "has it in" for Greece.

By her logic, the only food I could feel comfortable eating during a U.N. summit is from countries that are neutral.

Luckily, I like Swiss cheese and chocolate.

Though I'm sure it wouldn't be long before my mother would call to say "They just had a story on the news that cheese and chocolate can increase your risk of heart disease."

Then I'd be forced to eat *nothing* during U.N. sessions.

I'll be the only one on a hunger strike with no idea of what I'm protesting.

Halloween's not a big holiday for me. If I happen to hear of a party I'll go. But I basically outgrew Halloween when I was around twelve. Apparently, my mother is not aware of this.

"Boooo, Amila. Boooo. Okay, don't get scared. It's just me, honey. Tomorrow's Halloween, and I just want to warn you to throw out anything that looks suspicious in your trick-or-treat bag. Like if you should happen to find a hole in a candy bar, it could mean that someone stuck it with a hypodermic needle, all right? Happy Halloween, sweetheart. Bye-bye."

How could she even imagine me trick-or-treating at *this* age?

    (Knock, knock, knock.)

    "Who's there?"

    "Trick or treat!"

"My goodness! What a wonderful costume! Can you wait just a minute?"

"Actually, I'm not wearing a cos—"

"Staaaanley! Bring the camera! There's a little girl dressed as Jerry's friend Elaine! She has the hair and everything! It's amazing! She even looks like she's in her thirties!"

"That's because—"

"Your mommy must've spent quite some time making your costume!"

Other than the answering machine, which is her lifeline to me, my mother has some strong reservations about me getting involved with new technology.

"Hi, Amila. Y'know, it just occurred to me—what do you really need a laptop computer for? You'll spend a fortune of money to lug around a piece of equipment that really belongs in the home. It'd be the same thing as if you bought a scaled-down toilet to *shlep* around on a shoulder strap. And what if you get all *farmisht* and leave the computer on the table at a diner? It's like you're having an egg on a roll and leaving the waitress a three-thousand-dollar tip. So promise me you'll think about it, okay? Okay. That's that, I love you."

All right, here are the facts. At least 80 percent of this book was written on a laptop computer.

It was written in approximately thirty different visits to eleven different diners and coffee shops, without *a single instance* of my getting *farmisht* and leaving the establishment without my laptop.

And how could she even compare a laptop to a hypothetical shoulder-strap toilet? I don't think such a thing would ever see the light of day simply because people would never feel the same sense of pride bragging about a commode:

"Nice toilet, Bob! What model is it?"

"It's a PottyTech500 with a 2.4-gallon tank and a 3.2-inch chrome-plated flusher."

"Oh, man, I've been dying to get one, but I know the minute I do, they'll come out with the PottyTech 501."

"Yeah, it's hard to keep up with all the new stuff coming out of Porcelain Valley."

Okay, forget all these intellectualizations. I'm getting sidetracked. The point is, I'm an independent human being, and if I want to put my hard-earned cash into a laptop—if I want to walk into a diner and *hand it* to the waitress ("Thanks for the toast, here's a computer")—I should be able to do so without any flack from anyone.

*As a busy career gal, Amila never leaves home
without her Rush-and-Flush.*

My mother seems to have no faith at all in my ability to find my own dates.

"Hi, Amila. It's me honey. I was just watching the Maury Povich show, and the whole show was about eligible millionaire bachelors. And one of them in particular I thought would be perfect for you. He's a millionaire and he has a house in Italy. And I know how much you love spaghetti. So let me know if I should call the Maury Povich show, okay? Bye."

I called her back and told her, Absolutely do not call the Maury Povich show. Two hours later, I got another message.

"Yeah, hello, Amila, it's me again. I called the Maury Povich show and what would be required is to send the bachelor a video of yourself. So I had some thoughts. Like maybe you could put in a shot of you preparing a chicken. Or since they said he's such a big sports fan, you could show yourself by the TV yelling, 'Let's go Jets!' So call me back, *mamascheinz*."

- -

As for the first message: I thought one of the benefits of marrying a millionaire is that you *don't* have to eat spaghetti. I don't think anyone ever said, "I'd really like to marry a millionaire, so I can have a maid, travel the world, and dine every night on protein-enriched wagon wheels."

Now you may be thinking, "Wouldn't a mother as overprotective as yours have a problem with you running off to some guy's house in Italy?" Not at all. I think she'd be perfectly happy sleeping on his sofa.

And about that video: How could my mother possibly think *any* guy would be turned on by a shot of me preparing a chicken? Really, how seductive would it be to watch me yanking the pull-tab off a box of Healthy Choice?

What's Wrong with This Bachelor?

Despite my mother's enthusiasm for fixing me up with eligible bachelors, when it comes down to it, she knows what all parents know about their children: that nobody is really good enough for us. (This includes the doctor she *claims* to want for me.) The convenient chart below will save your mother the trouble of ferreting out the problems with your potential mates, since my mother's already thought of most of them.

Doctor: Works crazy hours, *shleps* home germs

Veterinarian: Works crazy hours, *shleps* home cat hairs

International businessman: Has woman in every port

Lawyer (civil): Too argumentative

Lawyer (criminal): Parolee could come after him with a gun

Artist/Actor/Graphic designer: Too bohemian, uses drugs, possibly gay

Computer/Internet professional: Downloads porno, *shleps* home viruses

Accountant: Won't know from you during tax season

Real Estate agent: Will put house in his name

Psychotherapist: Will blame all your problems on me

As much as I love my mother, we have very different ideas about how much time we want to spend together.

"Hi, Amila. It's me honey. I just wanna tell you, they're having some good airfares to New York, and I was thinking maybe I could come up for a little while. Like for a few months maybe."

Now while I'm sure that seeing me was the primary reason for her visit, the rest of her message revealed that she also had another very, very important reason for coming to New York:

"I have to go to that store on Third Avenue that has the pumpernickel raisin bread that I love. The only place that has it here has also, I don't know, like caraway seeds. Uchh. Feh. They gave me a slice, it made me so nauseous. Well, call me back, *mamascheinz.* Bye-bye."

My mother did eventually make the trip, but she only stayed for two weeks.

In Mom Time, that's a day trip.

As it turned out, "that store on Third Avenue" didn't exist, so off we went, *shlepping* on buses, trains, and foot, chasing down a bread that to my mother is the *specialty* of New York City. Apparently, I just wasn't aware that New York's nickname was changed to "The Big Pumpernickel Raisin Loaf."

While pumpernickel raisin *rolls* were readily available, it soon became clear that the Loaf Form would be a very, very rare find. We hit every bakery from First Avenue to Broadway, only to learn that most of them had never even heard of pumpernickel raisin in Loaf Form, let alone carried it.

Without really knowing what hit me, I found myself my mother's unwitting partner in a bread-finding mission that would span an entire city and ultimately prove to be a testament to the power of perseverance.

Not to mention a great source of personal embarrassment.

That night, she had me dialing my friends, dates, and business acquaintances to ask them, please, could they give me *any information at all* on where we could find a loaf. (I *had* to call, otherwise she would have called them herself, which would have been *twice* as embarrassing.)

But, alas, every trail was cold and breadless.

Refusing to accept defeat, my mother spent the rest of her visit asking *everyone* we encountered—cab drivers, neighbors, strangers on the street—if they knew where she could find some pumpernickel raisin bread.

Finally, as I hovered behind her, praying that nobody I knew would pass by and discover I was A Bread Addict's daughter, she leaned her head into a parked patrol car.

"Excuse me, Officer! Officer!"

"How can I help you, Miss?"

"Would you happen to know where I can find some pumpernickel raisin bread?"

"Some *what?*"

"Pumpernickel raisin bread."

"Did someone walk off with your loaf?"

"No."

"Was there a loaf illegally parked by your building?"

"No."

"Then sorry, I can't help you."

We returned to my building and, undeterred, she handed Gene the Doorman a ten-dollar bill and convinced him to scour the bakeries near his home in Queens, one of the few areas we had not visited on Our Mission.

Just when it seemed all hope was lost—when all neighbors, strangers, and public servants had failed—Gene appeared at my door and uttered the words that, frankly, I never believed I would hear in my lifetime:

"I found the bread."

Mom was *thrilled!* Victory at last!

There it was—tangible proof that *if one just perseveres,* no goal is too great to achieve and *no dream is impossible!*

I look back and wonder, long after most people would have given up, what fire inside kept my mother going? Was it a steadfast belief in a higher power? Or just a passionate, unrelenting desire to *nosh?*

Whatever obstacles you're facing right now, whatever detours are keeping you from achieving your dream, I sincerely hope that you, the reader, will draw some inspiration from this story of my mother's incredible journey.

Consider *this* your Pumpernickel Raisin Bread for the Soul.

People are always debating whether it's harmful for kids to watch too much TV, but I think the bigger problem is what happens when *your parents* watch too much TV.

"Amila? I just talked to you. Where'd you go? Anyway, I forgot to tell you—I was watching the news and they had a story about the Hell's Angels motorcycle club, and they flashed a shot of a big bear of a guy from Greenwich Village who was covered in tattoos, and on the back of his motorcycle was a very pretty girl, and I meant to ask, was that you? She had your hair, and she was wearing a green blouse that looked like the one that I gave you for Chanukah. I'm hoping it was just a coincidence, because you know how I feel about motorcycles. Do me a favor, Amy, if you have such ants in your pants like you wanna go for a ride, it can be just as exciting to go in a cab. Okay, keep your wits about you, honey. Bye"

First of all, my mother should know me well enough by now to realize I'm too much of a scaredy-cat to go flitting around town on the back of a Harley.

The last time I went for a ride in anything without a roof and four wheels was when my ad agency was pitching the Six Flags account. I discovered a lung capacity I never knew I had, letting off blood-curdling screams the entire ride.

And that was on the Ferris wheel.

I, of course, did understand her confusion when she saw the Very Pretty Girl's hair. There are *so few* women in Manhattan with brown, wavy hair that, really, who *wouldn't* assume it was me?

I'm *constantly* getting comments such as:

"Excuse, me, but I was just noticing how completely unique your hair is. What color would you call that?"

"Brown."

"Can you write that down? I want to ask my colorist about it."

With my mother, anything that happens to even a distant cousin somehow has an immediate bearing on my health.

"Yeah, Amila. It's only me. I don't know if you heard that Cousin Myron passed a kidney stone, and the doctors told him it's from not drinking enough water, which is why I'm telling you. Remember, honey, you're not a camel. They say that passing a stone feels like you're giving birth. And if you're gonna go through all that, I'd like to end up with something that can call me Grandma. Okay, honey, bye-bye."

There's no question that a baby would give her more pleasure than a kidney stone. I just couldn't see my mother—*any* mother—pulling an X-ray out of her wallet and bragging, "This is my grandstone Rocky."

But why does she always have to be so dramatic?

And the camel reference—I've had times when I've forgotten what day it was or couldn't recall my ATM number, but I've *never* stood there scratching my head, thinking, "Hmm, let's see, I don't have any fur so I can rule out *collie* . . . wild African boar is a possibility, but I'm looking in the mirror here and don't see a snout . . . hey, now that I think of it, I *hardly ever* get thirsty, and last week I *did* notice a little bump on my back—could it be that . . ."

I'm sure one of my mother's greatest joys was the first time that my nephew "J" called her Grandma. She's a proud grandmother, and her living room has enough pictures of him to pass for The National Museum of "J."

Now that I think of it, she's so loving, so proud, so maternal, that if I did end up producing her first grandstone, I just know Mom would find *some* way to brag about him: "Let me tell you, Myrna, little Rocky is so smart, he hasn't spent one minute in a classroom, and already he's been passed."

Whose Body Is It Anyway?

The last several years have seen intense controversy over who has the right to control a woman's body. Is it just the woman herself? Her legislator? Her doctor? Her god?

All the news stories and public debates have left out one very influential force.

Her mother.

Flip through this book and you'll see that my mother has attempted to control my bladder, my ovaries, my kidneys—even my boyfriends' *"shmekels."*

One of the worst parts is when I'm actually visiting my mother and she reminds me to go to the bathroom. In her sweetest little voice, as if she's talking to a toddler, she asks, "Gotta go baffroom?"

This is not just a problem for daughters; I got an email from a fifty-one-year-old man in Ohio who says that whenever he and his fifty-something brothers visit their eighty-three-year-old mother, she lines them all up in the bathroom hall to make sure that each of them "takes care of business and finishes the paperwork."

I think it's time the adult children of the world unite to reclaim our bodies from our mothers.

Take Back the Bladder, I say!

We'll raise funds with a concert— a Bladderpalooza!

We'll wear ribbons of toilet paper on our lapels!

We'll rally in Washington and *make our voices heard!* We'll make sure there are thousands of reporters! Hundreds of photographers!

And plenty of Port-a-Potties.

Fed up with mothers reminding them to use the bathroom, a mob gathers in Washington.

My mother seems think that, if she doesn't call me up to remind me of certain things, I'm going to lose all sense of time and space.

"Yeah, it's me, Amila. I'm calling to remind you to move your clocks ahead one hour tonight. So if you go to bed at ten, move the clock to eleven. And while you're at it, make a note in your appointment book that this year, February has only twenty-eight days. So don't go making any dates for February the twenty-ninth, because it just doesn't exist. All right, honey? Sleep well."

I do understand that my mother only wants to help me navigate the very, very difficult transition to Daylight Savings Time, when, as she puts it, "You'll have jet lag only you won't have gone anywhere on a jet."

But if she really sees herself at the Official Timekeeper of my life, shouldn't she be the first to realize that over thirty years have passed since I learned to tell time?

And as for the February twenty-ninth issue, well, she makes a good point—in fact, maybe I could use it to my advantage: "Y'know, Chuck, even though I've told you very nicely about seventeen times that I'm not interested, I'm glad you called again, 'cause I've decided I *would* like to have a one-night fling with you. Why don't I come over to your place on *February twenty-ninth*."

Really, messages like these are so irritating that, one of these days, I'm going to sit my mother down and tell her in very clear terms just to back off and quit calling.

Since I love her in spite of all her interference, I think I'll have that chat on September thirty-first.

My mother wants to make sure that I'm safe, from head to toe.

"Hi, Amila. I meant to ask you, the pair of shoes you said you bought, do they have crepe soles or regular rubber? Do me a favor, honey, it's very important: Check and see if they're rubber or crepe. Because they were just saying on the news that if you're ever in a plane crash, crepe is no good if you have to go down the slide. So let me know, okay? Bye-bye."

First of all, I've never even found *the airline's* safety instructions sensible, let alone my mother's. Take those plastic cards that show how, in the event of a crash, you should put your chest to your knees and scrunch your whole body into a ball. Now if you're in coach, aren't you already sitting that way?

The bottom line is, if my time is up and my plane's going down—from forty thousand feet at five hundred miles an hour—no body position, no life vest, and no plastic cup with a little rubber band is going to save me.

And as I'm crashing to earth and my life is flashing before me, I can't even imagine that my last thought would be, *"Oh my God! I'm wearing the wrong shoes!"*

Please. My last thought would be the same as that of any other young woman with hopes and dreams who suddenly finds herself strapped to a gurney in the ER:

"I hope I shaved my legs."

The last ad agency I worked for was located near Times Square, and a news story had my mother convinced there were a lot more things dropping than the New Year's ball.

"Amila? I just called your office and got your voice mail. I hope you're all right. I just saw on TV about the building collapse in Times Square, and I know that's right by you. They say the building wasn't occupied yet, but some elderly residents of a hotel got knocked out by the debris. So in case you have to walk by the building, you might wanna go to a sporting goods store and buy like a football helmet. That way, at least if you get hit by a falling brick, you'll have something to protect your little *keppie*. All right, give me a buzz so I know you're okay. I love you, honey."

I did give my mother a buzz so she wouldn't worry, but I told her I would not *for one second* consider purchasing a football helmet. "Mom, how could you even *suggest* that I parade myself through New York's prime business district looking like a New York Jet in drag?"

"What're you getting all excited for? There's deadly debris falling, and I don't think it's such a crazy idea to have something on your head."

"Yeah, but you want me to wear athletic *headgear* on the streets of Manhattan? That's insane!"

"No, it's not. Just go to any mall on a Saturday— there's not even any debris falling, and you know what?"

"What?"

"Half the kids are walking around in baseball caps."

*Taking a fashion tip from Mom, Amila stops traffic
in a hat inspired by falling debris.*

100% FOOLPROOF TIPS FOR HANDLING A MOTHER WHO CALLS TOO MUCH

will not be found here or anywhere else. Sorry.
You're just gonna have to learn to live with the aggravation.

• • • • • • • • • • • • • • • • • • • •

It seems like the end of this book is where I'm supposed to say something that'll give hope to other grown sons and daughters whose mothers use the telephone as a baby monitor.

Okay, here's what I have to say:

When you hear of something that works, let me know.

What follows are a few suggestions that were of zero help to me; but, since you were kind enough to get through this whole book and let me vent, the least I can do is offer them up and cross my fingers that you'll have better luck.

Suggestion #1

When your mother calls, tell her you're busy with something she'd *have* to approve of.

EXAMPLES:

◆ "I can't talk now, Mom. I gotta go get ready 'cause I have a date tonight with David Mermelstein, the *single doctor.*"

◆ "Thorry, but thith ith not a good time. I wath jutht in the middle of flothing."

◆ "I hate to rush you, but I'm trying to get to Macy's by six for their Semi-Annual Sale on Warm Sweaters, so can we talk another time? No, tomorrow's no good. I'll be busy all day eating roughage."

Suggestion #2

Agree upon a regular, predetermined day when you and Mom will talk.

Just pick whatever day works best for you—say, every Thursday or every Monday. Or, if your mom is especially challenging, agree to talk every Veteran's Day and *stick to it*.

This is what you can think of as Managed Irritation. *In theory,* with this strategy, your mother's comments, questions, and worries will still bother you, but it won't be quite so bad, since at least you'll know *when* it's gonna hit and you can do your yoga or take your medication or do whatever it is you need to prepare for The Conversation.

In reality, this is a little like prepping for a hurricane. You can board up your house, you can stock up on dry goods, but once the storm hits, it's *still* gonna put a major cramp in your day.

Of course, you really can't compare a mother's phone call to a natural disaster.

A mother's phone call is worse. For one reason: No matter how much damage is done, the government's not going to step in with relief. You'll never turn on the news and hear:

"The president paid an emergency visit to Manhattan today to survey the damage from Amy's last conversation with Mom. Her self-esteem was in shambles, and rebuilding her feeling of independence could take months. The president has vowed to provide federal aid to help defray the cost of therapy, which is estimated at twenty-three thousand dollars."

Suggestion #3

THE ONE-WORD RESPONSE The One-word Response is a parent-child communication technique that originated with five-year-olds. As in, "So how was school?"

"Fine."

"What did you learn today?"

"Nothing."

"Nothing?"

"Yeah."

At this point, the mother usually gives up, since getting a chatty response from the child is like pulling teeth.

The beauty of this technique in adulthood is that it allows you to talk to your mother and, without hurting her feelings, lets *her* be the one to decide the conversation isn't satisfying so *she* decides to end it.

I believe it's possible to have a conversation with any mother using only the following five individual words:

- fine
- yeah
- nothing
- okay
- chicken*

The fifth word is a good all-purpose response to any inquiry about what you ate or plan to eat.

However, I caution you against using this response to questions such as, "How was your day at work?" which would only alarm your mother and prolong the conversation.

*Occasionally, news stories will surface about bacteria-laden poultry, in which case you may substitute the words "macaroni," "brisket," or "stew."

Suggestion #4

Let your mother know that you screen your calls.

The idea here is, if she knows there's *a chance* you might be sitting by the phone screening, she has an Alternate Theory for why you're not answering to add to her collection, which most likely now includes:

(*Your name here*) is dead.

(*Your name here*) is in the emergency room.

(*Your name here*) was abducted.

She can now add a comparatively sunnier option, such as:

(*Your name here*) just doesn't feel like picking up.

Her feelings may be a little hurt, but at least it'll keep her from panicking. No mother, even mine, ever called 911 to say, "Hello, I'd like to report a daughter who's not in the mood to talk."

Suggestion #5

Ask your mother's phone company to adjust their rates.

If your mother lives out of town, one of the things that makes it all the more difficult is the outrageous long-distance phone rates. They're too low. Mothers are serial callers, and unless there's some deterrent, they're going to pick up that phone and do it again.

It's up to you to *take action*—write a letter or make a call—and demand that your mother's long-distance carrier abolish the nickel-a-minute deals and design a family plan that meets the needs of adult children. Here's what I think would be reasonable.

Monday through Friday, until 11:00 P.M.: $10 for the first minute, $35 for each additional minute.

Of course, after 11:00 P.M. weeknights and all day Saturday and Sunday—when you really need your personal time—the rates should be even better: $40 for the first minute and $100 for each additional minute.

It's a plan that would work for all parties: The phone companies would get richer, mothers could rationalize that we place a *really* high value on their calls, and adult children would finally have some peace.

Until the mothers caught on that with rates like these, it'd be cheaper to visit.

Suggestion #6

I was going to try to come up with a sixth suggestion, but then I had a scary thought: Could all this advice giving mean I'm turning into my mother?

GLOSSARY

Please note: This glossary will only give you a general "feel" for a word. Many of these words have various meanings, but I've only listed the ones you'll need to understand my mother's messages. If you happen to be a Yiddish scholar—which I doubt, or you wouldn't be looking up these words in the first place—please forgive me for not providing a more complete definition.

eppes: a *very* versatile word, meaning "well" or "maybe" but also meaning "really" and . . . well . . . *eppes,* it's hard to define.

farshtupped: all stuffed up.

feh: an exclamation indicating disgust.

farmisht: totally confused; probably how *you* feel reading these vague definitions.

keppie: head.

mamascheinz: sweetie-pie.

nosh: snack.

pish: to urinate.

plotz: to burst or explode due to overwhelming emotion.

shlep: to take a long, difficult trip. Also, to drag something.

shmegegge: a dopey guy or a nerd.

shmekel: penis.

shtup: an act that involves a *shmekel;* you can figure it out from there.

tuchas: buttocks.

DATE DUE

6.30.09			
GAYLORD			PRINTED IN U.S.A.